Jackie Devoy was born in 1964 in the inner-city Dublin neighbourhood of Fatima Mansions. With grit and determination, Jackie has lived her life by the creed that hard work can help you achieve anything, no matter your background. Though faced with barriers like poverty and limited access to education, Jackie has always forged her own path. After starting a family, she resolved not merely to survive but to thrive – living out loud, pursuing happiness without apology or worry of judgement. Jackie's inspirational story shows that circumstances at birth need not dictate the trajectory of one's life. By boldly going after what she wanted, Jackie found success on her own terms as a reminder that the human spirit cannot be contained by socioeconomic status. Both her struggles and triumphs stand as a testament to working tirelessly towards your boldest dreams.

I would like to dedicate this book to all the wonderful people I met on my dating journey, even to the ones with whom it never worked out. Without you, this wouldn't have been possible.

Jackie Devoy

The Joys and the Pitfalls of Online Dating

Austin Macauley Publishers™
LONDON · CAMBRIDGE · NEW YORK · SHARJAH

Copyright © Jackie Devoy 2024

The right of Jackie Devoy to be identified as author of this work has been asserted by the author in accordance with sections 77 and 78 of the Copyright, Designs and Patents Act 1988.

All rights reserved. No part of this publication may be reproduced, stored in a retrieval system, or transmitted in any form or by any means, electronic, mechanical, photocopying, recording, or otherwise, without the prior permission of the publishers.

Any person who commits any unauthorised act in relation to this publication may be liable to criminal prosecution and civil claims for damages.

A CIP catalogue record for this title is available from the British Library.

ISBN 9781035844791 (Paperback)
ISBN 9781035844814 (ePub e-book)

www.austinmacauley.com

First Published 2024
Austin Macauley Publishers Ltd®
1 Canada Square
Canary Wharf
London
E14 5AA

I would like to thank all the wonderful people who supported me and my dreams over the years, to Rachel Deasy, and to Austin Macaulay Publishers and their employees for their help, support and guidance in helping me get this book published.

Table of Contents

Introduction	11
Chapter 1: Before You Begin	12
Chapter 2: Internet Dating	14
Chapter 3: The Cheaters	22
Chapter 4: The Golden Years	27
Chapter 5: Newspaper Dating	34
Chapter 6: Face to Face	37
Chapter 7: Mrs. Yummy	41
Chapter 8: The Married Men	46
Chapter 9: The Younger Man	52
Chapter 10: The Time Waster	56
Chapter 11: My Thoughts & Tips	62
Chapter 12: Beware of the Paedophile	65
Chapter 13: Romance Scammers	69

Introduction

Well, before we jump right into the wonderful world of online dating and all it has to offer—the highs, the lows, or the joys and pitfalls, however you like to phrase it—dating comes with its own set of challenges and experiences.

Let me introduce myself briefly. My name is Jackie Devoy, and I am a proud, independent fifty-eight-year-old. I am a mother and a believer in finding a soul mate. I have been on first dates in Ireland, and I am the author of *"The Dublin Marilyn"* and *"The Enchanted Belle."*

In this book, I have endeavoured to share my stories, drawn from my own experiences and all that I have learned along the way. The content is based on my own true experiences, but the names, locations, and all other personal details have been changed to protect the identity of those involved.

Chapter 1
Before You Begin

This is the story of my experience with online dating. Some of my experiences are good, and others not so great! While online dating has become a significant part of life in the 21st century, it comes with its own set of fears and challenges.

We all know some people who have had great success in meeting their significant other through online dating; however, not everyone has been so lucky. I would like to share all about my experiences and what I've learned on my dating journey. I aim to share this in my own words, hoping my sense of humour shines through in telling these stories.

From my own experiences, I've come up with a few do's and don'ts that might benefit some of you who are about to set out on your own dating journey, or perhaps you're already on that road. Who knows, you might still find these useful.

1. Don't stare at men or talk too much.
2. Don't meet him halfway or go Dutch on a date.
3. Don't call him and rarely return his calls.
4. Always end telephone calls first.

5. Don't accept a Saturday night date after Wednesday.
6. Fill up your time before the date.
7. Always end the date first.
8. Stop dating him if he doesn't buy you a romantic gift for your birthday or Valentine's Day, etc.
9. Don't see him more than once or twice a week.
10. No more than casual kissing on the first date.
11. Don't rush into sex.
12. Don't tell him what to do.
13. Always take the lead.
14. Don't expect a man to change or try to change him because he won't.
15. Don't open up too fast.
16. Be honest but mysterious.
17. Don't date a married man.
18. Always look after yourself and look well.
19. Be easy to live with.

Chapter 2
Internet Dating

With the dating profile created… and the picture uploaded!

It's not long till I get notifications on my phone… Bing! John likes your profile… Bing! John would like to chat with you…

So, with a mixture of nerves and a lot of excitement, let's see what John has to offer. It politely kicks off with the usual chit-chat:

(John) "Hi, how are you doing today?"

I replied, "Hello," keeping it cool!

(John) "So tell me about yourself, what are your memories all about?"

I said, "Tell me yours?"

John replies, "Well, I travelled the world and met many lovely people along the way," and he told me all about the birth of his two daughters and how he saw them grow up and fly the nest.

"Now it's your turn," he said to me.

"Well, I am delighted for you travelling the world. I hope you are well. What do you want to know about me? Are there things you want to know or don't want to know? If so, ask me, and I will tell you."

I said, "What do you do in your life that enables you to travel the world?"

He said, "It's your turn about your memories."

"Okay, so I'll begin… Well, I am working in a hospital. I have children. I am divorced, and I live in Dublin. I have a film being made into a book next year hopefully, and I am currently looking for funding for a new book I am working on. I hope to get it soon. I have another book published, so I am keeping myself busy," I said in a light-hearted way.

I continued to ask him about his experience of travelling the world.

"Do you love it? It would not be my 'cup of tea,' but I hope you are enjoying it."

John then showed an interest in me and asked questions about my book.

He asked, "What is the name of your book?"

I happily told him it's called *"The Dublin Marilyn"* as in Marilyn Monroe. I grew up in inner-city Dublin when most people were poor back in those days, when some women had fifteen children, possibly even more, and the church would not help them. The book will be out there in three weeks' time. Then I continued to tell him the other one is a film going into a book that I need funding for (not thinking too much of it), "Wish me good luck on that one," I said.

He said, "You need funding? How much?"

I replied, "Oh, it's big money, about 4000 euros. Really hope someone helps me with it. I am a positive thinking person, so I believe it will happen."

I then tried to put the attention back on him and asked him, "Are you happy travelling the world? Why are you on a dating site when you could probably meet the woman of your dreams sitting on a boat or an aeroplane?"

I started to think to myself that I don't think I would be on a dating site if I was travelling the world. Anyway, to each their own, I suppose. I'd be happy just going to the countryside.

John replied with, "How if he could give me half the money now and half in a month's time but I would need to pay him back if he was to give it to me."

He asked, "When could you pay it back?"

I said, "It is a lovely thought John. Thank you so much, but I don't know when I could pay you back. So, I would just rather leave that at that because I don't like pressure on my head. I might not be able to pay you back until I get my royalties back on it. I just don't like to feel under pressure like that. It is not good to have pressure on my head or shoulders. It's so nice of you to offer me the money. Thank you so much. But I will probably get a sponsor from somebody, hopefully soon. Wish me well on that one; you are so kind."

I was keeping it respectful, well so I thought.

He said, "So you don't want me to help you? That's okay!"

So now he is asking me for more new pictures of me. I said I don't know how to send them. My friend helps to put me on the dating site and create my profile. I asked John if he had WhatsApp.

John replies back, "And you said that you were writing a book, ha ha ha. You must be mad…ha"

So I explained how I never went to school much, so I wouldn't be great with computers. But yes, I have written a book! I have dictated it. The technology is wonderful, and yes, of course, I have written a book. Just because I did not go to school much doesn't mean I can't do things. I am a very clever woman, and you shouldn't be so quick to judge. You shouldn't knock anybody; your English is not great either. And by the way, there are people who went to Trinity College and cannot even spell properly, for your information. And you should not judge people; you won't be laughing at me when I'm going all the way to the bank when I become a millionaire. We will see who will be laughing at me then. This man did not believe me; imagine him thinking I was a scammer!

I told John my friend was here, and I would talk later; I needed a break from him. A couple of hours later, I got a message from him.

"Now you can send me an up-to-date picture?" So I did.

"How old do you think I am?" I asked.

He said something like twenty years older than my actual age…

So, I replied, "The cheek of you… I am nothing near that age."

He said, "What age are you?"

I said, "I'm fifty-eight, but I only look forty." He said, "Who told you that?"

I replied, "Everyone that knows me!" He said they were probably only being nice.

I went on to call him a very serious person, and he replied, "I believe everything I see and only half of what I hear."

I said, "John, I think you're getting Alzheimer's disease. I will look after you when you come to the hospital." He then sent me a picture of an old man saying, "The years have been good to me." The man in the pictures looked about 100 years old.

I said, "Imagine meeting him on a blind date; I'd be gone like the clappers." He said something out of a scary movie. (We were getting on well chatting back and forth, having banter.)

He asked, "What if this old man was a millionaire?"

I said, "He could keep his money because I'd be gone like the clappers."

He said, "That's my dad…" I was in a heap laughing at him. Now this is all texting; we haven't spoken on the phone yet.

John asks, "Do you like jokes? You have a great sense of humour."

He said, "Oh, you should do an audiobook?"

I sent him pictures of my old house that I had done up in Clondalkin. It's full of Marilyn Monroe memorabilia (if you google it, you will see it).

He told me it looked like something you'd see in Las Vegas. He asked me if I was looking for a manager; I told him I don't need a manager.

John went on to say my spellings are very bad. I might not have gone to school much, but I'm a fairly clever woman. I continued to tell him about my struggles and experiences in getting a book published in Ireland.

I said the Irish publishers are very hard to get in contact with, and they seem to not want to give you a chance, so I went to London to a publisher called Austin Macaulay. They are one of the biggest publishing companies you can go to.

"If I could get someone to sponsor me, it would be nice." He said, "How much do you have in the bank?"

What a question to ask, I thought to myself.

I said, "About five thousand euros, why?" He asked, "How much do you need to publish your book, and when will I get it back from you?"

I already told him I don't need his money. I have an editor helping me, a lovely professional Nigerian man.

He said, "I don't like the sound of a Nigerian involvement. They are all scammers!"

"Okay, it has been said before that the majority of them are, but this man is cool and not like that. He has helped me get a number one book out there; I am happy with him.

"I work with a lot of Nigerians at my job. You cannot just paint everyone with the same brush! There are a lot of Irish scammers too, so you can't just say that. You don't even know the people."

He said, "You have been warned; I wouldn't trust any of them, so as the dragons say… *I'm out, I won't be investing.*"

I said, "I never asked you for money for my book."

He then goes on to say, "It's hard to trust any woman over the age of fifty."

"Why would you say that?"

He said, "Talking to them and meeting them."

I said, "They are not all the same; you can't be saying that. They are not all the same."

He said he'll try to stick to the under-fifties. I said, "You should try the over-seventies."

He goes, "When the Nigerian takes all your money, you will look seventy!" Ha ha ha.

In my opinion, this man is a big fool. He asks me how many times I have been married. I said, "What type of question is that to ask a lady?" But I answered anyway. "Once," I said. I then asked him how many times he has been married.

And I was shocked when he replied, "I don't want a woman; I want a slave!"

I said, "I wish you well on that one."

He said, "I wish you well on your book; be on good watch out for the scammers."

I said, "I work with nice Nigerians and all foreign nationals; they are not all scammers. I did not think he could shock me anymore, but I was wrong."

He said, "I disagree with you; I don't like Niggers."

"And what would you know; you don't work with them, and you should never use or say that word! And I hope you don't ever need someone to take care of you!" I continued to say to him, "You are very brown yourself? Is that out of a bottle? Would you like to be black?"

I said, "I would not mind being black." He called me a NIGGER lover.

I said, "Your personality stinks! You don't even know me! You are desperate!" I told him to go back on the site and give someone else your disrespect because I won't be taking it anymore.

He said, "I don't care what you do, you Nigger lover; you are a big fake."

I said, "You are the image of my delete button."

He said, "That's definitely not black, so." I just never answered him again. How disgusting and disturbing was he! You have to be careful on these sites.

Sweet Buffalo

He is eighty-five years old and insists on taking his wife's hand everywhere they go. When I asked him why his wife kept looking away, he responded, "Because she has Alzheimer's."

I then proceeded to ask him, "Will your wife worry if you let her go?"

He replied, "She doesn't remember anything, she doesn't know who I am anymore. She hasn't recognised me for years." ('Heartbreaking,' I thought to myself.)

I said, "And you have continued to guide her every single day, even though she doesn't recognise you."

The elderly man smiled and looked into my eyes and said, "She may not know who I am, but I know who she is, and she is the love of my life."

Now, that is an example of true love! That is a gentleman!

Chapter 3
The Cheaters

So here are some random phrases or pickup lines you might see on these dating sites.

- I came across a couple in Crete looking for a sister wife – just three people sharing a relationship together. She is not bisexual or a lesbian but would love a sister/best friend.
- They love coffee and Netflix, discreetly looking for drama-free hook-ups.
- Life is about taking chances and not giving a toss about what people think.
- Looking for fun, excitement, and passion.
- "I am in an open, honest relationship, which allows each other to have different relations/partners."

It's sad for people who find out their partners are cheating on them after years of marriage; it's terrible. Do they not recognise the damage they will cause? Do they not realise that it will all start falling apart, on both sides of the fence? Both families will fall apart, and their children will be devastated. What is wrong with these people? If you don't love your partner, leave them. You cannot have the best of both worlds; it is not possible! Kind, compassionate, fun, non-judgmental are the words of a man, who then continues to tell me, "To be very honest, I have been married to an incredible woman for over 20 years, but the intimacy is gone. I crave intimacy and I really miss it. Not all affairs are illicit. I've tried everything, but she is no longer interested. I appreciate it sounds bonkers, but it is the truth and I don't want to lead anyone on here. I will send pictures on request!"

Is he an honest man?
Is he a cheat?
Will he find someone on this site?

Next up, we have…

Jay:

One man said, "Life is too short, so make the most of it!" A stonemason single man looking to date but nothing too serious. He said, "Hi, I won't be here too long. I think I'm bored, I need someone to spend my money on!"

Mick:

"I am not going to bullshit you, I am looking for a casual thing if I'm honest, and I'd rather be called a dick for telling the truth than be called a liar just to get into your knickers."
 "Hi, Mick, I appreciate your honesty, but no one was getting into my knickers!"

His reply: "No worries, happy HUNTING."

I replied, "I like your style, but some people's knickers are bigger than others, if you get my drift. Good luck on your search. PS: I hope your dick doesn't fall off while you're looking through the site."

Mick replies, "Nothing wrong with big knickers, the bigger, the better, and there is no fear of my dick falling off…"

I said, "There is when syphilis is all over the site," and he goes, "That's what condoms are for."

Doctor Paul:

Doctor Paul was a divorced man who wanted a relationship, seeking a woman for a long time, not just a fun time.

 "I said hello…"

Dr Paul: "Hello Jackie, you look very sexy! Fancy a coffee?"

Me: "Where are you from?"

Dr Paul: "I now live in Wicklow."

Me: "I live in Clondalkin. Why do you have no pictures up?"

Dr Paul: "Because of GDPR, I've been advised not to put them up. I see you are healthy, are you a nurse?"

Dr Paul: "Could we play doctors and nurses? And do you wear high heels and black stockings?"

Dr Paul: "Or could you wear high heels and stockings?"
Dr Paul: "You look like a prostitute…"

Move along there, Doctor Paul, that's if you are even a doctor at all. I don't normally reply to men who have no picture up on the site.

There are a lot of paedophiles on these sites or married men, and then you have the men who are simply just looking for sex! Scumbags you have to look out for; you have to be careful. Some of these men have problems in their lives, someone that is going to use and abuse you, so you have to be careful. You have to do your research, look at their profiles, and be clever. After you have done that, you won't be easily hurt. If you're going on a date, make sure to do your research, try to stay ten steps ahead of them.

You have to be confident. You have to know what you like and what you don't! If you don't like them, get up and leave, tell them you are going to the toilet, or if you're a smoker, even better, go and keep walking… Don't go back, good luck to them. Some of the men on these sites are in bits, have no haircuts, long and scraggy, grey, and I even came across a few with no teeth, and they think they are so beautiful looking.

"If you put them in a bath of acid they still would not be clean."

But then you have the men who overdress; you need to be careful of these men too. They tell you that they are from Dublin, but really they could be anywhere – America, Africa, India, Brazil, anywhere!

They put up a faux profile picture. In my experience, I found it to be a picture of a white male, claiming to be Irish. But they sometimes forget that you can check on WhatsApp.

I once video called a man who was African American, sitting in his living room drinking.

The house was in bits… and he would sit there and say, "Hello pretty," trying to sweet talk me and convince me he is a millionaire. Absolute scammer… You have to look at their appearance and attitudes, listen to the questions they are asking you.

Look for them asking you what you work at, if you live on your own, have kids, and if they live with you. If you say you do not work, they ask you questions: How do you feed yourself? What money do you live on in life?

You have to look at all the pros and cons; you have to try to be smarter than them. I am not trying to frighten you, but you have to be careful not to be fooled by these men. They prey on the weak.

If you see an international number, please beware, this is very likely to be a scammer! I would put money on it! Remember never to give your personal details out like emails, postal addresses, or dates of birth.

You'd be surprised what these scammers can do with your information!

Chapter 4
The Golden Years

As you get older, time starts to fly. One foot over the hill, you can hear it whiz by. Your sight starts to fail and your hearing starts to go.

You will probably swap your high heels for more comfortable shoes, your luscious dark locks turn platinum grey, and when gravity shifts, your body parts stray.

Those once perky little boobs that sat high on your chest now hang out with your tummy under your vest, your bones creak when going up the stairs, and you can now cough, sneeze, and pee at the same time.

Everything aches, and your muscles won't flex; your libido left at home along with the sex life you once had. Your teeth in a glass when it's time for bed, and when you wake in the morning, you are relieved you are not dead.

Your once lovely freckles become liver spots, and you will forget everything as your memories are shot. You get shorter each day, but strangely, your ears and noses will continue to grow, your joints will be stiff, and your hips a bit achy.

When sipping your tea, you will notice your hands might be shaky, you might get arthritis in the elbows and knees, and you struggle to walk to the kitchen without starting to wheeze. Only haemorrhoid cream can relieve the pain of constipation's daily strain!

These golden years will come to us all, when the thrill of the week is the bingo hall. I really should not moan; it could be much worse. After all, I am still here and not yet in a hearse. Marriage is like a deck of cards.

In the beginning, all you need is two hearts and a diamond. By the end, you wish you had a club and a spade! Don't only look for a pretty face; it will turn old one day.

Don't look for soft young skin; it will wrinkle in time. But do look for a loyal heart that will miss you every day and love you forever…

Be aware:

Do not fall for a man that asks for money. Don't be fooled by the sad story or the promises; if he asks for money, be cautious. Many people have been scammed and never got a penny back! I have said it once, and I will continue to tell you to listen to what they are telling you, read in between the lines.

When dating a man or woman that you met online, you need to make sure you do your research, look at their profiles, and again listen to them.

There might be clues/warnings to if they are married or a scammer? Or hopefully, you will find someone genuine! You could be all dressed up and excited to go out, and they won't answer you or call you back.

They could be meeting someone else or playing games or, worse, just wasting your time. They play the site, and sometimes they end up calling a few days/weeks later. Be careful if you decide to give this person a second chance; I would not recommend it! I would say some people have a great laugh, while more people will unfortunately shed tears! So I was on Plenty of Fish, or some people call it POF for short. This man said hello to me, so I said hello back, and that was it. The next morning, I got a message from a woman who said that was my husband you were talking to last night.

I explained to her that I just said hello, but to be honest, I was angry about why this woman was texting me. So I told her to go back through all his messages and look and see if he actually met up with someone, but it wasn't me so don't text me again.

If he is cheating, just throw him out and get rid of him; for what he is doing to you, it is not me you need to be arguing with or talking to; it is him. If I were her, I would walk away from him because in my experience, I don't think he will stop doing that to her.

I also believe she needs to look at her relationship and why is he online chatting to other women.

- Is he unhappy, and why?
- Is he seeking connection?
- Is he lonely?
- Is he just looking for sex?

Sometimes relationships go stale, so you need to stop and look at your life and see if it can be fixed. Either by spicing things up or rebuilding your communications/connections. If, after doing this, you should look at the relationship to see if it's making you happy or time to call it a day. Some things I feel are important to remember:

- The past cannot be changed.
- Opinions don't define reality.
- Everyone's journey is different.
- Judgements are not about you.
- Overthinking will lead to sadness.
- Happiness is found within you.
- Kindness costs nothing.
- It is okay to let go and move on.
- What goes around comes around.
- Things always get better with time.
- Never look back; you're not going that way.
- Live a happy and healthy life.
- Always look for the positive.
- Take care of yourself; self-care is everything.

I am talking to a couple of men on Plenty of Fish; one man's name is David. He claims to be 5'11" in height (180cm). David is from Athy and is fifty-nine years old. David's profile reads like this:

"First of all, I am not an up-to-date member. Hello to you all and happy New Year. I am hoping to find that special someone who follows their dreams. I like being outdoors, but I have been letting it lapse in the last few months, so send a message and let's see where this takes us. I don't really want to be a pen friend, so serious people only. Let's see where this gets me."

He socially drinks, has kids, and a dog. His interests include walking, music, DIY, golf, and learning ukulele. So, I texted him, and he texted back:

David: Hello Jackie, how have you been? Are you new to the site? I know it doesn't sound great, but I have been on it since before Christmas. COVID has been a great success for not meeting someone? Have you had much luck?

Me: Hi David, yeah, I'm no stranger to the site. Have you had much luck yourself in meeting someone?
David: Yes, I've met a few lovely ladies and even stayed friends with a few of them. You?
Me: Yes, I've met a few people, but a lot of people are not nice here.
David: Well, I'm here now.
Me: So, David, what do you do?
David: I am a trained killer, retiring this year. Just sold my house and have been looking for a nice woman to spoil for a few years. Fancy a world cruise?

I was laughing to myself, just as I was about to reply, he rang me, and we talked and made arrangements to go out. So the next day, when I was getting ready to go out with him, I texted him; no answer. I called him; no answer. So I sent him a message saying, "If you knew you couldn't make it, you should have let me know! I turned down my friend today because I thought we had plans."

David replies and said, "I said 'if,' Jackie. Take care and stay safe, goodbye." This is what I mean when I say you need to listen or read in between the lines. Another one, the image of my delete button. All people have to do is say that they're not going to be able to make it.

Detective Dickie:

His profile reads like this: fifty-eight-year-old detective, professional, I have a master's degree. 6 foot (185cm), separated, looking to date but nothing serious.

Easy going, straight-talking kind of fellow, happy and positive. He claims to be a gentleman, a good listener. Enjoys hillwalking, hugs, and talking.

Looking for a woman who is a working professional, like-minded, enjoys the outdoors, comfortable with life and with mine.

Apologies for not having any photographs up, I sometimes put them up when online, but they're always available, just ask.

Nothing sinister about not having them up, just don't fancy leaving them up there when I'm not actively online.

He writes at the end of his profile, you know what, the half-empty glass is always refillable.

So I decided I would text him:

Me: Hello Richard, How are you?
Richard: Just having a WANK! Want to help me!

How can anyone go out with this man and call yourself a gentleman! Needless to say, I won't be texting him back! People on dating sites claim they want to go on dates, but they don't!

Chapter 5
Newspaper Dating

Fifteen years ago, dating sites were done through ads in the newspaper. I remember getting the Herald Newspaper and seeing they had a dating page. To respond or set up a profile ad, you needed to get an inbox number, and in order to do this, you had to pay money. There might have been a way to do it for free, but I didn't know how, so it ended up costing me one hundred euros.

Once I was all set up and the Herald had my details, I started to receive phone calls. One evening around six o'clock, I got a call from a man. His name was Paddy, and he told me he was from Cork.

He confided in me, sharing that he was a gambler and an alcoholic. We chatted for a while that night, and he said he would call me back tomorrow at the same time. He did, and this pattern continued for months.

As we got to know each other better, he improved at communicating. He had cows and would feed them when he got home from the pub. Sometimes I could hear him talking to them. He seemed like a harmless man, just looking for company.

He gave me the impression that he was a lonely man. Sometimes he didn't know what to say, so I would do all the talking.

Over time, I noticed his communication got better with me as he became more comfortable. He told me he did not want a girlfriend, but I think he never had one, to be honest.

He loved to talk about inventions and was passionate about them. Paddy told me about how he and his uncle invented a golf machine, and that it was nearly ready.

He talked about watching Dragons Den on television every Thursday, and inventions were one of his favourite topics. He was an inventive person, and his uncle was an amazing man who had tried to invent many things.

His uncle passed away, so his son took over the golf machine business. I hoped it would happen soon for them and wished them success on their journey.

I've been talking to Paddy for about fifteen years now. After five and a half years, he asked me for my bank account number, and I was shocked.

I thought about it, but he reassured me, so I did. I went to the bank the next day and asked the teller about my account balance. She said there was nothing.

A few days later, I went back, and there was nine and a half thousand euros! I was in shock and couldn't believe a man I never met would do that.

I asked Paddy why he did it, and he said he felt close and grateful to me because we had talked every day for years.

About six months after that, I went to Tipperary to meet Paddy. We went for something to eat, had a pint of Carlsberg, and I even had the pleasure to meet his auntie. She was a lovely Tipperary woman, and we had coffee while she shared stories about Paddy and her nursing days.

Paddy and I will always be best friends. The ads are no longer in the Herald anymore; they are all online now. Frank texted me on the site, telling me how before internet dating, he put an ad in the newspaper:

"Single man looking for a wife or a companion."

He said he received numerous replies from men offering their wives. So here I am, I thought I would give it a go, he tells me. He seems like a genuinely nice guy, so we are chatting back and forth.

I asked Frank to tell me about himself, and he replied, "Well Jackie, what can I say? I am handsome and the greatest man alive, and the mirror blushes every time I look into it." He was funny.

I shared my newspaper dating experience, and he went on to say that just like the dating sites, genuine people are rare. "What's rare is wonderful, but if you don't try, you will never know."

Chapter 6
Face to Face

Meeting people face to face is a different experience from talking online or over the phone. It's not easy, and you might have a good or bad experience.

Before meeting, I recommend chatting with them for a while, doing a social media search if possible, and letting someone know where you're going – safety first.

Allow me to share a couple of my face-to-face dating experiences.

John, a solicitor from Balinteer, and I chatted for a few days before deciding to go on a date. He picked me up from Clondalkin, and we went for a drink at the Clarion Hotel.

He came across as pleasant and polite, asking what drink I'd like before heading to the bar. After some good chats and a couple of drinks, things seemed fine until he asked about booking a room for the night. I was devastated.

Why did he lower the tone like that? I declined, saying I'm not that type of lady. He then said he was only testing me. Later, he showed me a picture of a beautiful girl from his wallet, explaining she was his ex-girlfriend.

They still lived together until she found somewhere else to live.

Realising how badly the date was going, I took a large sip of my drink and asked why they broke up. He, a fifty-year-old father of four, didn't want any more kids because he felt he was too old.

His ex, a thirty-five-year-old Polish girl he met online, believed he was okay with having more children initially. Now, two years later, he changed his mind, she's angry, and they don't talk anymore.

I told him I don't blame her and that I think he's being selfish. He asked if I thought he was too old, to which I said it's his body, and no one can tell him what to do.

He offered to drop me home, and I got out of the taxi, saying goodbye. About an hour later, he rang, saying he doesn't think we'll be going out again.

I thought, *You got that right!*

I once went on a date that turned into a counselling session. He wasn't a bad man, just confused and in need of someone to talk to.

Who knows, he might become a dad again. But I wonder what would have happened if I had said yes to the hotel room?

Another time, I was talking to Tom, an accountant, and things seemed promising, so we decided to meet.

We met outside the GPO in Dublin city centre, and he looked nice. We headed to a pub for a pint, and as I sat waiting, time ticked by. I finally asked the bar boy to check if there was someone at the bar. It turned out, the man had walked out of the door! I was puzzled.

He was forty-five but looked much older than me despite me being ten years older. He probably hoped to meet an older woman and wasn't sure what to do, so he ran! You wouldn't want low self-esteem with these men.

Then there was the man I met in Lucan, who I like to call Normal Wisdom because he was funny.

We met outside Kenny's Pub in the village. When I said hello, he looked in my direction, and I wasn't sure if he was looking at me, the wall, or someone else – he had a lazy eye.

He went to the bar to get drinks, and as he walked, I noticed he tripped over his own feet. He was the funniest. He took out his comb and started fixing his hair, saying he had to look good for me.

I burst into laughter like a hula hoop. As the night went on, and we had more pints, he sat down and accidentally knocked over his drink, fretting over his new shoes getting soaked. I couldn't help but laugh.

He was very clumsy but hilarious. He made a great effort for the date, but despite him making sure I got home safely, I didn't want to see him again.

Albert Einstein is widely credited with saying, "The definition of insanity is doing the same thing over and over again and expecting the same results."

Thanks to my dating site experiences, I'm starting to see what Albert meant. So, it's time to change or explain why I've used these proverbs to describe myself.

About me:

My name is Jackie, and I'm tall, around 6'2", with a good build, although I've eased off the gym under chiropractor's orders.

Not something that bothers me; I know I can bounce back. I'm not a heavy drinker, enjoying the occasional pint, an ice-cold beer, or a glass of wine.

But the social aspect matters more. I don't smoke. I have a grown-up daughter, and we have a great relationship.

I adore animals; my beloved dog passed away, and I adopted three cats that became part of the scenery.

I'm easy-going, with a good sense of humour. I enjoy dining out, musicals, and love trying new things.

Now about those proverbs:

I believe in reaping what we sow and treating others as we wish to be treated. I find solace in books; they offer a world of imagination.

One of my favourites is "A Garden Carried in the Pocket." Imperfections make us who we are, and each generation reaps what they sow.

I advocate for education and independence and embrace the importance of learning from mistakes.

As the old Chinese saying goes, "They who ask the question look a fool for five minutes, but those who don't ask look a fool for a lifetime."

I believe in facing fears; if it scares you, it might excite you.

These mantras and phrases are integral to how I live.

Chapter 7
Mrs. Yummy

So, I came across a profile that caught my eye. It was short and sweet; his name is Sean, five foot eight in height, from Foxrock.

He's fifty-five, a professional, highly educated, with no children – single and seeking a woman for dating. We matched on the site and began chatting.

Sean: Hi Jackie, I'm Sean. Nice to meet you. How are you finding the dating site?
Me: Hi Sean, I'm good thanks. There's all sorts on this site, but I haven't met anyone genuine yet. There are a few scammers; you need to be careful.

Sean: Ahh sure look at it, I have nothing to scam anyway. But I am afraid of the ladies who proposed an hourly rate! I have to say they declined. I'm not that desperate.
Me: Well, not yet, give it a week.
Sean: It's been a while, Jackie…
Me: Well, I don't charge, ha ha ha.
Sean: That's good to hear. You're mad.

Sean: Tell me a bit about yourself, Jackie. I really like your smile and your style.

Me: Awh, thanks Sean. I'm from Clondalkin and work in a hospital. Have you been on a dating site for a long time?

Sean: Only since Saturday. I'm just a rusty guy trying to start dating again. Are you dating much?

Me: About three months, but as I said, it's hard to find those who are genuine.

Sean: You are yummy.

Me: What type of woman are you looking for on here?

Sean: Oh God, I've only just arrived and I'm still trying to figure the app out. Let's see – attractive, funny, smart, sane. I think the same as most people. What about you, Jackie?

Me: Awh, the same as yourself, Sean. Absolutely someone funny, a good communicator, with a nice personality.

Sean: I think you're yummmmmmmmmm…

Me: 😊

Sean: I'm teasing you, Miss Yummy. So, what do you like to do for fun in your life?

Me: I say you are alright, you big tease. I work in a hospital. What about you?

Sean: I have a small business but right now, I'm in bed on my own.

Me: Bad night was it? What happened, couldn't you sleep?

Sean: I came back for an hour and decided to look at your profile. But how can I sleep after looking at those pictures? Very sexy.

Me: Now, be nice.

Sean: You are sexy and you know it. Do you have WhatsApp? Can I get your number?

Me: Yes, you can have my number, but you have to be nice, LOL.

We moved from the dating site and started talking on WhatsApp.

Sean: So, are you modelling, Jackie?

Me: No, I'm not a model. But I was on First Dates Ireland two years ago. You can catch it on YouTube or the RTE Player.

Sean: Do I really want to see you dating other guys?

Me: It was a show my friend entered me in. Watch it.

Sean: We could watch it together if we go on a date.

We continued to chit-chat back and forth, discussing our jobs, hobbies, and what we liked to do outside work. He seemed nice, asked if he could call me, and we talked on the phone.

But it seemed to fizzle out, so we said goodbye. Was he genuine or a time-waster? I'll never know. But I wish him well exploring the site.

Another man, Keith, texted me on the dating site. He was forty-four, living in Dublin – a good-looking man, I have to say.

Keith: Hello, I've seen you on First Dates. You're extremely yummy; you must get that all the time.

Me: Hi Keith, yeah, that was me. My friend signed me up for the show. What did you think of it?

Keith: I fancied you then on the show, and I think your photos are yummy now. You are one sexy…

Me: Awh, thanks Keith. That's nice of you to say. Where are you from?

Keith: I mean it, Jackie. You are hot. I'm from Blanchardstown. You coming over to see me?

Me: Ha ha, you wish! What are you up to?

Keith: At home looking at your pictures. Do you like younger men, Jackie?

Me: It depends on the man and his personality.

Keith: Well, I'm a good lad, love a pint and a bit of craic down the pub. I'm laid back, real easy going. I would love to take you out for a date, Jackie. Would you be interested in a guy like me?

Me: Yeah, sure, we'll see what happens. I like to get to know the person a little more before meeting them. Tell me about yourself?

Keith: So, not only are you yummy to look at, but you're sensible too. I'm a carpenter, work hard during the week, and like to have fun on the weekend. I'd say you're lots of fun.

Me: That's good, Keith. Have you been on the site long? Had much luck?

Keith: On and off for a few years. Yeah, I've gone on a few dates. Sure, that's what it's for, right? So yummy Jackie, will you come on a date with me? Can I ring you?

So, I gave him my number, and he rang me. We chatted for a while, and it turns out he was married.
After chatting, he admitted it and said I was his type. He thought I was extremely good looking and so yummy. But I am not a homewrecker.
 When karma comes back to punch these cheaters in the face, I'd like to be there in case she needs a hand.

Chapter 8
The Married Men

It's incredibly worrying and disturbing to see the number of married men on these sites. Some of them disclose their marital status, while others keep it concealed.
Are there women who go along with these married men, knowing they're married? That's not my cup of tea… No way!

I received a text from Bernard, a fifty-nine-year-old from Dublin, saying, "Hi beautiful, how are you? I must say, you are gorgeous.

"I'm in a loveless marriage and looking to date. I would love to take you out and then I would fuck you." He had no photos. Who do these men think they are?

"Image of my delete button"

Jeff;

One day, I got a text from a man named Jeff.

"Heya, how are you? I saw your profile and thought, O.M.G she is one sexy lady. Would you be interested in an indecent proposal or €€€, totally respectful. Discreet with no strings attached but most importantly lots of fun."

Ehhh, no thanks, Jeff. Prostitution is not my idea of fun! But after a little research, it turned out this man was married. I wonder if his wife notices his strange behaviour or if he's just that good at sneaking around!

That level of disrespect is disgraceful. Well, I hope she catches him and packs his bags.

Karma's a bitch, Jeff.

The next man was Tom. On a Thursday night around eight-thirty, my phone went off.

"Hello there, Jackie. How are you? I hope all is good with you. I'm new here, and I have to say, you look great."

I replied, "Thanks, how are you?" He continued to compliment me, "You have beautiful eyes. Why only one photo up? Would you send me more?" He had none, of course.

So I asked him, "Why do you have no photos?" Turns out, he was married and all he wanted was fun. I can't deal with men like that. Why do they marry if they want to cheat? Does sex mean more to him than his wife?

I received a text from a man who didn't give his name and had no picture up. He texted me, "You are definitely not fifty-eight! You look absolutely stunning." I asked him why he had no pictures.

He said, "I am not single, I am married, and I just want to have a bit of fun with a good looking woman." What's wrong with these people?

I know I keep saying it, but I'm shocked at the number of men out there disrespecting their wives. Where have all the good men gone? The gentlemen? Are there any left?

On these sites, not only do you have to deal with scammers, married men, and time wasters, but you also have to deal with the young ones, barely old enough to drink, the ones with fetishes, or those who simply want to use you for hook-ups or self-pleasure.

I received a message from a man called Kaig, a taxi man. We had the usual chit-chat, and he asked me out. I wasn't feeling it, so I declined, suggesting we could still be friends. He asked me if I thought he was ugly.

I said, "No, you're not. We are all different, and what one person finds attractive, someone else might not." He then asked if I was looking for something different. I said yes but found him very handsome.

He asked again if he was too young for me. I gently tried to let him down by saying yes, but we could still be friends and talk. He asked if I would do him a favour. I said okay, but it depends on what it is, LOL.

He asked if I would chat with him tonight as if I was interested in him, and after tonight, he would never bother me again.

"I just find you very sexy, Jackie," he said. "I will be honest, I am in bed alone, and you make me very horny. Sorry, you are just so beautiful, will you indulge me just for tonight?" He sent me a dick pic, LOL.

He wanted to pleasure himself while I was talking to him. And trust me, he is not the only one out there doing it. I swear the site can get crazy! So be careful.

On these sites, you come across all sorts of men. These men are so full of themselves, writing things like:

Ste:

Forty-four-year-old male, active, fully vaccinated, ready to shift, married with three kids, looking for some side action, discreet fun. Drop us a mail if you're interested.

Pat:

Fifty-one, employed, fun-loving, outgoing, married but looking for fun, excitement, and a lady he can be himself with. (His words)

When Pat mailed me, he said, "Hello, gorgeous, how are you? I would really like to get to know you, maybe we could hit it off and have some fun."

I would like to say I was shocked, but the truth is the longer you stay on these sites, the less shocking they become. So I replied, "Hi, Pat. I think you're looking in the wrong place. I have no time for cheaters. Maybe put the effort you're putting into this site into your WIFE! I would love to know what his wife thinks of this."

James:

"Discreet woman required. Regular lover, maybe you want me every now and then, don't be shy, say hello."

Alex:

"Life is about taking chances and not giving a toss about what people think. Looking for fun and excitement with lots of passion. I am your man. I am in an open honest relationship which allows for each of us to have different relationships."

Ron:

Ron was a frothy 41-year-old, two kids, separated as he claims, but still living at home with his wife and children, looking to date.

Ron mails me and tells me all about himself, how he loves his children, and how the breakdown of his marriage was so hard on him.
But now he has to pick himself back up. He describes himself as a gentle, cool man, easy-going, and fun-loving.

Funny how these men describe themselves as easy-going, fun-loving, honest. If you ask me, I would describe them as dirty pigs, dishonest creatures, thinking with their dicks, and trying to fill their egos! Selfish.

The list could go on. His poor wife or ex-wife, if he's telling the truth, probably hasn't a clue what's going on right under her nose.

I reckon more than half the men on some of these sites cannot be trusted. Either they're cheaters, scammers, or time-wasters.

Well, that's my experience anyway. There are too many men out there who are being dishonest to their other half. It is actually unbelievable the number willing to do that to their partners.

The good ones are few and far between. Thinking the grass is greener on the other side, it will all end in tears, and hopefully, it will be theirs!

Chapter 9
The Younger Man

You would not believe the number of younger men seeking older women. The confidence in these men would shock you, well, it did me anyway. Some in their twenties texting me.

   Is it just for sex?
   Are they scammers?
   Is it for a laugh?
   Is it a weird fetish they have?
   A fantasy they want to fulfil?

Or is it for real? Are these men genuine? I cannot get my head around it. Here are some of the men who reached out to me on the sites, and remember I am 58 years old.

Joseph:

"Twenty-seven-year-old male, from Dublin, working professional, single, never married."

Joseph: Hey there! How are you sexy? So, I reckon you could find me useful... A younger man in your life to have some fun with.

Me: No thank you, Joseph.

Joseph: Are you sure, Jackie? Like, it would be great fun!

Me: Joseph, my son is older than you!

Joseph: Aw, sure if you wanted to, we could even just have some fun while we wait to find someone our own age? Let me know, I promise you won't regret it.

Like, is he for real? The confidence in this man! Chancer...

Fionn:

"Twenty-two, single, college student, from Galway, fun, easy-going person."

Fionn: Hello, you look like a goddess. Would you be interested in having a twenty-two-year-old sex slave? I am ready and willing to be used and abused by you. I would do just about anything for you. Just say it! I would like to lick you, starting at your toes and working my way up!

Well... I never replied...

"Image of my delete button"

Connor:

"Twenty-four, male, from Sligo but living in Dublin, looking for a mature lady to date. C.E.O of my own company, I work hard but that's okay with me, I enjoy what I do and love to succeed.

"When I am not working I love to travel, my favourite place is the south of France. I like eating out, wine and a good restaurant, nothing like sitting in a romantic candlelit restaurant with a good bottle of wine facing an interesting and attractive woman.

"My ideal woman would be someone that dresses classy but sexy, intelligent, has a good sense of humour and doesn't drink too much and fall over.

"Life is here to be enjoyed and there is nothing better than having the right person to share these intimate moments with."

Connor: Good evening, Jackie, you look beautiful in your pictures. I would really like to get to know you more. Would you be interested in getting to know me?

Me: Hi Connor, I'm well thank you, but I think you might be a bit young for me.

Connor: Jackie, when I looked at your profile I thought you looked like a classy lady who would enjoy all that I have to offer, read my profile Jackie! Age is just a number.

Me: Hi Connor, I do believe age is just a number in some circumstances, but everyone has their limit and I'm afraid you are way too young for me.

Connor: WELL, it is your loss, Jackie… You should never judge a book by its cover! I am a successful businessman that could change your world. If we hit it off, I would have brought you places that you could possibly only dream…

Can we take a moment for this arrogant man! I did not even reply, but I do wonder, is this a real person? Or is he a scammer? A little keyboard warrior, all text and no bit lol.

Chapter 10
The Time Waster

Along with the younger men, the cheaters, and the scammers, we have the time wasters.

These men like to lead you on, make you feel like they are serious, that they will bring you out on a date. Are these men bored, or are these men scammers?

John: Hi, I like your photos, very nice, you are a very good-looking woman. I'm John, and I am from Anglesey North Wales in the U.K. I live near the ferry port, where the boat comes in from Dublin.

Me: Hi John, it was nice to get your text, I hope you're having a very nice day.

John: Yes, I am, thanks. I spent the day with my son. How are you? Tell me a little about you?

Me: What would you like to know?

John: The important stuff lol… Like, have you married, do you have children, etc.?

Me: Hi John, yes, I've been married a long time ago and yes to children; they're grown now. What about you?

John: Yes, I have three children, two boys and a girl. I got divorced because my ex-wife cheated on me. When I got divorced, my boys came to live with me as they did not want to live with their mother and her new partner.

Me: That must have been hard for you, John. Are you from Wales?

John: Ah, it was, Jackie, but you get over these things in time… No, I was born in Dublin but left school at fifteen. I became a bricklayer. I could have built my own house but instead, I joined the Royal Marines and travelled all over the world.

We seemed to have hit it off; the conversation was easy, and we texted back and forth on the app for a few days.

I asked if he wanted to call, and he said he did not have the code or the phone number to be able to call from England to Ireland.

Would you believe that…? Needless to say, I did not hear from him again.

#timewaster

Carter:

So, one day, I got a text message from someone I was talking to before.

"Hello Jackie, how are you doing? It's Carter Delaney from the site."

So I replied, "I'm good, how about you? How come you have an American number?"

"I have a house in Phoenix, Arizona, in the United States. I mostly live here and travel around the world."

"Oh, I see. Is that why you went silent?"

He replied that he was busy with work and then showed great interest in my work.

"Are you still working in the hospital? Did you work through the pandemic? Gosh, that must have been difficult and tiring."
"I missed talking to you, Jackie," he said.

We chatted back and forth for a few days. He told me he was coming to Ireland soon and asked if I wanted to meet. I, of course, said yes, no problem; we can get a drink or a coffee when you are here.

Later that day, my daughter came over, and I was busy chatting with her and not on my phone. I got a message from him asking, "Why didn't you write back? Were you busy talking to other GUYS!"
I explained I was just busy, and he said, "Phew, because I was getting worried, you didn't like me."
He then asked if he could ring me and have a proper conversation and plan his trip when he comes back to Dublin.

Later that night, we were talking, and I knew he did not sound like the white man in his pictures, so I took a moment and just listened.
He questioned me again about my work and the long days, etc. He asked if it was a well-paid job.
I decided I was going to call him out on this. How dare he! "I know you are a scammer!"

"I know you are not white. I know you are coming on this site to rip me and other women off! I won't be dealing with you! Goodbye!"

You have to be so careful. And as I said at the start of this book, listen to what they are saying and how they are saying it, and never give out your personal details.

I feel like if I was not aware of this scammer, he would have tried to love bomb me and tell me he was coming to see me, and when they have you excited, an emergency happens and they ask you for money! So be careful.

One fella called John texted me and said, "Good morning Jackie, this texting thing is useless, better to meet in person, don't ya think? Are you on WhatsApp? Send me your number, and we'll arrange a date." He never got back to me, saying one thing and doing another!

#timewaster

I like to talk to someone on the phone for a while; I find this is the best way to get to know them before you go through the effort of meeting them.

You get to hear their voice. Do you like the sound of it? Can it be trusted? You get a sense of their personality.

Does the conversation flow? Does it feel natural, and you feel comfortable?

If the answer is no to any of these questions, my advice would be not to go. It's too much effort, and you're probably going to get hurt.

I was talking to this man on a dating site for nearly a year. He was telling me how he was an entrepreneur and that he has houses in Belfast, Malahide, and one in Florida. He stays in Malahide on weekdays for work and spends the weekends in Belfast. He works for a computer company in Dublin City Centre.

He asked me out a couple of times, but he could never collect me. I didn't like the idea of that; I believe men should collect you and drop you home. Old-fashioned values.

He texted me three months later and asked again if I would meet him in Mcgovern's restaurant in Malahide. So again, I asked him to collect me. He said he couldn't because he wanted to have a glass of wine. He told me to get a taxi, and he would pay for the dinner and drinks.

So, I got a taxi over; it cost me 70 euros from Clondalkin to Malahide. When I got there, he was opening a bottle of wine. I noticed when he was pouring the wine, he half-filled my glass but filled it to the top.

We ordered our food; he ordered a seafood platter, and I just ordered a burger and chips. I started cutting my burger in two and asked him if he would like some.

We were chatting away and enjoying our time. He told me he was staying in a hotel around the corner and would I like to join him for a drink?

I told him that it was too soon for that, so we headed for a drink in a pub down the road.

He ordered a Bombay Gin while I was drinking a pint of Carlsberg. We had a laugh, but I could sense he was pissed off. I wouldn't go to the hotel with him.

When we were walking outside, he said, "Are you sure I can't twist your arm to come have a cheeky drink in the hotel?" *(Does he think I was born yesterday?)*

I politely said, "No thank you," again and told him it takes more than a dinner and a few drinks to get me into bed!

He laughed nervously and said, "There is your taxi."

Earlier in the night, I was telling him how expensive my taxi was, but it seemed to just roll off his back. This self-claimed, well-off man, with his three homes, was not going to put his hands too deep into their pockets if he wasn't going to get something out of it for himself!

I have a few words I would like to call this man!

Chapter 11
My Thoughts & Tips

So, as I said at the start, this book is based on my experience of online dating, the ups and the downsides of it. While I was active on the sites, I learned a few things I hope will help you on your dating journey. I'd like to share my thoughts on what I've seen and experienced online.

To me, it's funny how some people will want to abuse you, then have the nerve to act like they are the victim. So be careful and keep an eye out for this type of gaslighting behaviour! A man who cheats or beats his wife is not a man in my eyes; a man should use his strength to protect his family, not hurt them.

Be careful when you're looking for your knight in shining armour, so that you don't get fooled by them and end up with a horrible person. I used to rush to defend myself against false accusations, but now I watch to see who believes it. This way, you know who to cut off first! Don't let anyone who hasn't walked in your shoes tell you how to tie your laces!

Some people are like birds; you help them to fly and once they are in the air, they shit all over you. The biggest mistake I made is letting people stay in my life far longer than they deserve. Ladies remember, a leopard can't change his spots! You see a person's true colours when you're no longer beneficial to their life.

I will admit I have my flaws and imperfections; we all do. Mine are that I love too hard and I give too much too fast. I can either give up too fast and run, or I'll stay too long and fight too hard for something I probably just walk away from. But you live and you learn.

Knowing your own self-worth is key and never settle for less than you deserve. I never went with a married man; it is a complete NO for me. I wouldn't do it and I wouldn't like it to be done to me. I don't understand why women blame other women when a man has an affair; yes, women should not do it, but the man should get the blame.

I believe when a man has an affair once, he will do it again, even if he promises you the earth. I think if a man thought he could get away with it, he would do it again, and how easy is it for them now with these dating sites? All honesty, respect, and most importantly, trust would be gone out of the relationship. The relationship will never be the same again; as they say, a leopard cannot change its spots! He brings nothing but stress, worry, and headaches!

A man can treat a lady right for one night, but it takes a great man to treat her right for the rest of their life. I believe most of a man's success has a lot to do with the woman he chooses to have in his life, and some will know and respect this, and some will ruin it for everyone.

Strong women aren't born. They are created by the storms they had to walk through from others in the past. For relationships to work, you need to give your partner the respect they deserve, be honest, and carry yourself with dignity at all times, and vice versa. It takes two to make it work.

Chapter 12
Beware of the Paedophile

For most of us, signing up to online dating sites is to find a match, someone to date, talk to, or even hook up with. Yes, we have cheaters and time wasters!

We even have to keep an eye out and beware of the scammers. But never in a million years did I think this would be a platform for paedophiles. It's hard to spot these men, and unfortunately, they don't wear a sign on their heads.

These men could come across as decent men; they might even have been married before and have children or families of their own.

We all know the terrible outcome if something were to happen to a child. The poor child would be robbed of their childhood and never be the same again. A huge number of families fall apart because of these men or should I say monsters!

> We have to be on guard and responsive to this, keeping an eye on your children's phones or devices. Be selective about the men you bring home or introduce to your children. Do your research on the

men you meet on these sites because they can be telling you anything over the phone.

It sickens me to share this story, but I think and hope it might be an eye-opener to any single mothers out there. I was talking to a man on a dating site, and he seemed really nice.

We chatted back and forth, the conversation seemed relaxed and was flowing nicely. He asked me if I had any children, which is a typical question when getting to know someone.

I replied yes, I have a daughter. He continued to ask how old she was, and I innocently answered him.

But I noticed he was asking lots of detailed questions about her: her name, school, how she got there, her appearance. These questions were hidden behind his chatting and flirting with me.

When I dodged the question, I started to notice he would ask it again. It made me question why he was showing such an interest in my teenage daughter, and it was no longer in a friendly getting-to-know-you manner. He even had the audacity to ask if she was well developed!

My gut told me this was not right, so I told him to stop texting me and called him out on his sick ways. I reported it to the site. It's crucial to look into his background before bringing them near your home or children.

Paedophiles use these sites to meet single women with children. They'll try to love bomb you and might be more cunning, making it harder and more dangerous for us. So, please remember to do background checks, look them up on other social media sites, and Google their name. Stay one step ahead of them.

After researching and talking to other women about their experiences with online predators, the general feedback is that when these men start talking to women, it's clear they are seeking single mothers.

They almost seek them out and, when they find one, these predators show keen interest, almost love bombing them. They make the women feel special, comfortable, and believe they've found a good guy.

These men can be eager to meet you. In many cases, dating a single mother comes with childcare challenges, and these men know this. Often, they'll say things like:

> "Bring them, I love children."
> "Bring them, I am great with children."
> "I really want to see you, because I really like you, tell them I am your friend."

They might even joke about being their uncle. None of us want to think like this, but my advice to you would be:

- Look up their names extensively on Google and all social media sites.
- If they're very keen on meeting your children, pull away or better block them.
- Take your time before introducing them. Remember, the right man will be understanding and patient.
- If you do introduce them, don't leave them alone.

- Listen to your children and what they have to say.
- Listen to your GUT! A woman's intuition is always right.

I'm not saying all men out there are paedophiles just because they show an interest, but I am saying stay alert.

If you're interested in this and the Irish justice system, keep an eye out for my next book.

Chapter 13
Romance Scammers

Internet dating is known for the scammers—these people are called Romance Scammers. They create fake profiles on dating sites, apps, or contact you through social media sites like Instagram and Facebook.

The scammers often start a conversation and build up your trust, engaging in frequent conversation multiple times a day. There are signs to identify an online scammer:

- The scammer is quick to fall in love.
- Their profile will be vague.
- They will lack other social media pages.
- They will swiftly ask for money citing emergencies.

Some scammers exhibit luxurious lifestyles or hold respectable jobs. Then, there are those who love to bomb you, emotionally leaning on you, narrating their struggles, hoping you develop feelings and offer to transfer money.

Tyron

Tyron texted me on a dating site, claiming to live in a grand house in Las Vegas. He mentioned being a widower, his late wife succumbing to cancer.

I replied, "Hi Tyron, hope you're well, sorry for your loss." He expressed delight that I messaged back, praising my beauty and readiness to move on.

But as the conversation progressed, I began to suspect he was lying or a scammer. Curious, I decided to see where this would go and played along.

Tyron spoke of wanting to remarry, working for the US Marine Corp in Afghanistan but due home in three months. As we chatted, he detailed plans to move to Dublin, start petrol stations, and promised gifts like a beautiful diamond.

After several days of flattering compliments and promises, Tyron messaged after a silence:

> "Good morning, my love. I've been unwell and need an operation, but my money's tied up in a gas station development. Can you help?"

He likely assumed I'd fall for his ploy and offer money. Sadly, many women fall for these scammers and never recover their money. I called him out as a scammer and deleted him.

I've encountered numerous scammers on these sites, reflecting in the plethora of books and films based on people's true life experiences.

I spoke with a well-educated man on the site who highlighted that it's not just men scamming women; women can also scam men. These women may catfish men for a place to live, money, or even a passport. They might have husbands in their home countries.

He shared a personal experience of arranging a date with a woman who turned out to be vastly different from her picture and identity. This disheartened him and made him cautious on dating sites.

Pat:

"They're fine, but a lot of people can't tell the truth about their age."

Anto:

Anto shared a story about meeting a girl for coffee. When he arrived at the coffee shop, a woman approached him who appeared to be a size 24, vastly different from the slim girl in her picture. He didn't want to leave abruptly but felt uncomfortable. He politely offered her a coffee, but she declined, suggesting they go to her place nearby, hinting at wanting sex. Anto, feeling degraded, left as she lied about being single and her appearance. Women on dating sites come and go—conversations might start and abruptly vanish without explanation.

Karl:

"Some crazy ones and a few nice ones, but it's hard to tell what they really look like because of the filters."

Darren:

"I met a girl on the site from Romania. We talked for weeks, even video chatted, and planned for her to visit Ireland. However, she encountered a family problem and asked for money. Friends warned me and an online search revealed many red flags. It was a close one for Darren. Men need to be cautious on these sites too."

Dario:

Dario messaged, "Hi, my dear, my name is Dario. I live in America and work in mining for diamonds. I plan to retire and relocate to Ireland. My wife and children died tragically in a car accident years ago. Now, I seek a partner to take care of and be taken care of by."

There was something off about this man, but I wanted to hear more.

Dario: What are you doing today?
Me: Hi Dario, I'm just working today, and you?
Dario: What do you work at?
Me: I work in a hospital. What about you?
Dario: Are you a doctor?
Me: No, I'm not a doctor, I just work in a hospital. What do you do?

This was where he told me about his mine and diamond business.

Dario: Do you own your house?
Me: Yes, I do.
Dario: Oh, you will have to sell it and come to America to get married to me. I have a big house that you can live in.
Dario: I cannot wait to have and see my new wife.
[Dario sent me a picture of a bunch of flowers and wrote, "Until the day I can hand you a real bunch, these will have to do."]
The next day, Dario texted again.
Dario: Hello, my wife. How was your day? Did you get something to eat?
Me: I did, Dario. I had my dinner.
Dario: What did you have? Did you go to mass? Did you say your prayers? Because that's important to me.
[Dario sent another picture of flowers]

"To my wife, good night and God bless."

Me: Thanks and good night.

The next day, I woke to more flowers and a text asking me what time I finish work and he would call me.

I told him eight o'clock. He continued to send love hearts and flowers throughout the day, little messages like "thinking of you," "cannot wait till you're my wife." When I finished work, Dario rang me, asking what I will do now for the evening, what I will have for dinner, how he misses talking to me when I am at work.

I woke up to a "good morning, wife" text and a picture of a bunch of yellow roses. He told me he was working down the mines today so he won't be able to contact me, but he has to go down and look for diamonds so he can give it to me when we get married.

A few days later, I got a message from him, saying, "Hello wife, I found a beautiful diamond today and I'm going to give it to you." He told me he loved me and asked why I wasn't calling him my husband.

I was at work one day and I did not pick up his call. I got a message from him saying he is worried about me and he needs to know where I am at all times. He told me he found more diamonds and wants to come visit me in Ireland soon, and he is going to look after me. He told me I won't have to work anymore; he will have enough diamonds to take care of me.

He continued to tell me he loved me and sent loads of flowers. He said he was nearly finished with this job, and once he's done, he will have loads of money and diamonds and is coming to get me and take care of me.

One day I got a phone call from him, "Hello, my wife, I have bad news, my machine broke and until I can fix it I won't be able to retire, I won't be able to come to you. My darling wife, I am suffering. I don't think I can live like this anymore. I think I want to die unless I can get the money from somewhere."

I woke to a picture of a bunch of flowers and a message saying,

"Wife, I need you to send me the money to fix my machine, I need it soon. I will pay you back and I'll give you more money back, but if you love me and don't want to upset me, you will help me. I cannot live like this, I need you before I die."

This scammer worked hard, but he was not successful this time.

Image of delete button lol.